Rookie Read-About™ Science

Thanks to Cows

By Allan Fowler

Consultants:
Robert L. Hillerich, Ph.D., Bowling Green
State University, Bowling Green, Ohio

Mary Nalbandian, Director of Science,
Chicago Public Schools, Chicago, Illinois

Fay Robinson, Child Development Specialist

 CHILDRENS PRESS®
CHICAGO

Design by Beth Herman Design Associates

Library of Congress Cataloging-in-Publication Data

Fowler, Allan
     Thanks to Cows / by Allan Fowler.
        p. cm. –(Rookie read-about science)
     Summary: A simple description of how a cow produces milk and how
the milk is processed for human consumption.
     ISBN 0-516-04924-0
     1. Dairy cattle–Juvenile literature. 2. Cows–Juvenile literature.
[1. Dairying. 2. Milk. 3. Cows.] I. Title. II. Series: Fowler, Allan.
Rookie read-about science.
SF208.F68 1992
636.2'142–dc20   91-35062
                                                       CIP
                                                       AC

These cows live an
easy life.

They have a nice clean barn to sleep in on their dairy farm.

They have a beautiful
meadow to graze in,

plenty of water to drink,

and plenty of hay, corn,
and other good things
to eat.

In fact, a cow eats her food twice.

After swallowing her meal, she brings it back into her mouth, a little at a time, and chews it more slowly.

This is called "chewing her cud."

Although their life is easy, cows earn their keep.

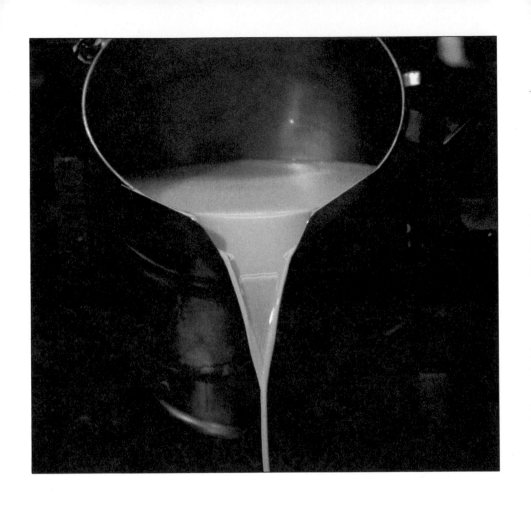

A dairy cow gives about
80 glasses of milk a day.

Cows are adult female cattle.

Holstein cows are black and white. They give the most milk.

Jersey cows are usually tan.

And there are other
breeds of dairy cattle.

A cow starts giving milk
after her first baby, or
calf, is born.

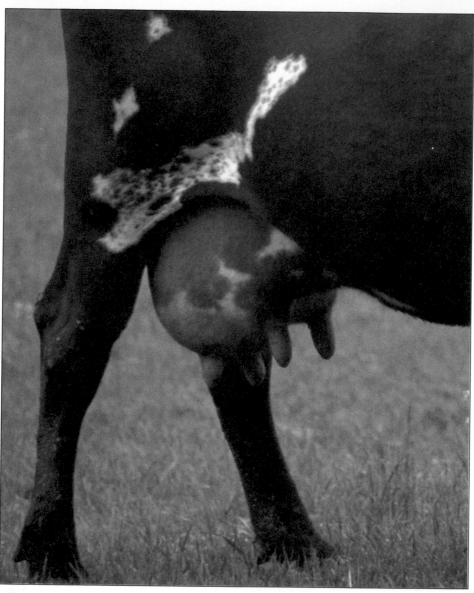

18

Milk collects in the cow's udder, a bag that hangs from her body.

There are four teats on the udder.

The milk flows out when each teat is gently pulled and squeezed.

Farmers used to do this by hand.

But on large dairy farms today, the cows are milked by machines.

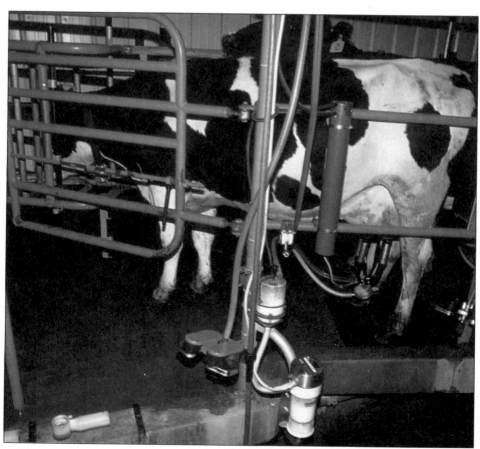

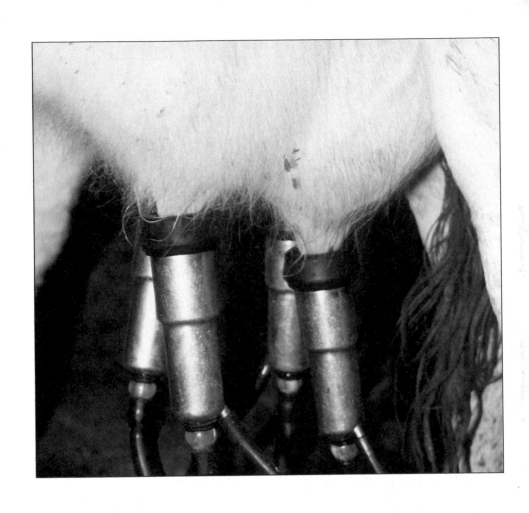

Each cow is milked twice
every day.

Trucks with big tanks
carry the milk from the
farm to a dairy plant.

There the milk is heated,
or pasteurized. This makes
it safe to drink.

Some of the milk is used
to make butter, cheese,
and other dairy products.

So you have a lot to thank cows for... especially if you love ice cream!

Words You Know

cow

calf   udder   teat

barn

hay

30

breeds of dairy cattle

Holstein

Jersey

Guernsey

Brown Swiss

dairy products

ice cream

sour cream   milk   cheese
butter   cottage cheese

Index

About the Author

Allan Fowler is a free-lance writer with a background in advertising. Born in New York, he lives in Chicago now and enjoys traveling.

Photo Credits

American Dairy Association® – 11, 25

Animals Animals – ©Henry Ausloos, 9

PhotoEdit – ©Myrleen Ferguson, 4, 30 (bottom left);
©Tony Freeman, 27, 31 (bottom left)

SuperStock International, Inc. – ©Conrad Sims, 17, 30 (top right);
©Donald A. Curtis, 23

Tom Stack and Associates – ©Brian Parker, 22

Valan – © J.A. Wilkinson, Cover, 3; © Phillip Norton, 5, 6 ;
© Kennon Cooke, 7, 30 (bottom right),31 (center left); © Chris Malazdrewicz,
12, 31 (top left); ©K. Ghani, 13, 31 (top right); Val and Alan Wilkinson, 14, 31
(center right); ©V. Wilkinson, 15, 29, 31 (bottom right); © Michel Julien, 16;
© Jean Bruneau, 18, 30 (top left); ©Karen D. Rooney, 21

COVER: Ayershire cows